9/11—WHAT A DIFFERENCE A DAY MAKES

JAMES W. MOORE

9/11

WHAT A DIFFERENCE

A DAY MAKES

DIMENSIONS
FOR LIVING
NASHVILLE

9/11—WHAT A DIFFERENCE A DAY MAKES

Library of Congress Cataloging-in-Publication Data

Moore, James W. (James Wendell), 1938-
  9/11-what a diference a day makes / James W. Moore.
    p. cm.
  ISBN 0-687-03049-8 (pbk. : alk. paper)
  1. September 11 Terrorist Attacks, 2001. 2. Terrorism—Religious aspects—Christianity. I. Title. Nine eleven-what a difference a day makes. II. Title.
  BT736.15 .M56 2002
  248.8'6—dc21

                                        2002001876

All scripture quotations, unless noted otherwise, are taken from the *New Revised Standard Version of the Bible,* copyright © 1989, by the Division of Christian Education of the National Council of the Churches of Christ in the United States of America. Used by permission. All rights reserved.

Those noted RSV are from the *Revised Standard Version of the Bible,* copyright 1946, 1952, 1971 by the Division of Christian Education of the National Council of the Churches of Christ in the United States of America. Used by permission.

Those noted NIV are taken from the *Holy Bible: New International Version ®.* Copyright © 1973, 1978, 1984 by the International Bible Society. Used by permission of Zondervan Bible Publishers. All rights reserved.

02 03 04 05 06 07 08 09 10 11—10 9 8 7 6 5 4 3 2 1

MANUFACTURED IN THE UNITED STATES OF AMERICA

In loving memory of all the innocent people who lost their lives on September 11, 2001

CONTENTS

INTRODUCTION

The phone call came early on Tuesday morning, September 11, 2001. "Turn on your television," the caller said. That scene repeated itself all over America. All over our nation and our world, people tuned in to the breaking news about the terrorist attacks. People everywhere were stunned, shocked, heartbroken, and grieved as we tried to comprehend what was happening. News correspondents were trying frantically to "get the story" and give us the facts.

Sadly the story unfolded. Four planes had been hijacked by terrorists. The World Trade Center in New York and the Pentagon in Washington, D.C. had been attacked, and another hijacked plane had crashed in Pennsylvania. There had been horrendous devastation and loss of life. It was like a Tom Clancy novel, but it was not fiction; it was painfully, agonizingly real—a horrible, tragic nightmare that set our world reeling and broke our hearts.

How could this happen?

What does this mean?

Who is responsible?

Why would they do this?

Is it over?

How do we respond?

How can we help?

These questions and others flooded our minds. But my mind also darted back to the Scriptures, to some verses I had learned in Sunday school as a child. I recalled the words of Jesus in the Gospels. He said, "In the world you have tribulation; but be courageous, for I have overcome the world" (John 16:33, paraphrase). And later he said, "Lo, I am with you always" (Matthew 28:20, paraphrase).

That's what we hold on to—both then and now. That's what we continue to wrap our arms around. That's what we stand upon: the promise of God to be with us always, the promise of God to give us courage, the promise of God that God's truth and righteousness will prevail, the promise of God that his goodness will overcome evil and his light will vanquish the darkness. So, trusting God to be with us, we go on with life, grateful for every moment we have, recognizing how fragile life on this earth can be and realizing what a precious gift life is.

In the book *Barbara Cartland's Book of Useless Information* (London: Corgi, 1977), Cartland wrote that when the Mona Lisa was stolen from the Louvre in Paris in 1911 and was missing for two years, more people went to stare at the blank space on the wall in the museum than had gone to look at the great masterpiece in the twelve previous years! There's a message there somewhere, and I think it is this: Sometimes we fail to appreciate precious things while we have them. We tend to take things for granted. Only when one of these precious things is taken away do we become painfully aware of the "blank space" in our lives and then focus sharply on that blank space. The walls of our lives are crowded with magnificent "Mona Lisa" paintings—freedom, church, family, friends, loved ones, and so forth—but too often we take these precious things for granted.

"I have often thought it would be a blessing," Helen Keller once wrote, "if each human being were stricken blind and deaf for a few days at some time during his early adult life. Darkness would make him more appreciative of sight; silence would teach him the joys of sound" ("Three Days to See," *Atlantic Monthly,* January 1933). The events of September 11, 2001, broke our hearts and dramatically prompted us to reassess our priorities.

Do we take our blessings for granted?

Do we take our freedom as a nation for granted?

Do we take our individual freedoms for granted?

Do we take our church for granted?

Do we take our faith for granted?

Do we take our loved ones for granted?

I hope and pray that we will stand tall—now and in the future—and go forward with life, celebrating our blessings, celebrating our freedom, and celebrating our faith, knowing that God is with us and that nothing can separate us from him and his love.

1

WHEN YOU ARE UNDER ATTACK

Psalm 139:7-12

September 11, 2001, is a date that we will remember for the rest of our lives. It is ironic, eerie, and sad that the way we write that date numerically is 9/11. On that Tuesday morning, our nation and our world took a blow to the heart as terrorists hijacked U.S. commercial jetliners and crashed them into the World Trade Center in New York and the Pentagon in Washington, D.C.

It was a ruthless, vicious, hateful, fiery, coordinated attack—one that stunned our nation, shocked our world, and killed thousands of innocent civilians. The news was so horrendous that the *Houston Chronicle* used two large headlines to trumpet the lead story: "ASSAULT ON AMERICA" and "TERROR HITS HOME."

Here's how it happened:

At 8:45 A.M. (EST), American Airlines Flight 11, carrying ninety-two people from Boston to Los Angeles, crashed into the north tower of the World Trade Center.

At 9:03 A.M., United Airlines Flight 175, carrying sixty-five people from Boston to Los Angeles, crashed into the south tower of the World Trade Center.

At 9:30 A.M., President Bush called the crashes "apparent terrorist attacks on our country."

At 9:40 A.M., for the first time in our nation's history, the Federal Aviation Administration grounded all flight operations. All inbound international flights were diverted to Canada.

At 9:43 A.M., American Airlines Flight 77, carrying sixty-four people from Washington to Los Angeles, crashed into the Pentagon. Trading on Wall Street was called off.

At 9:45 A.M., the Capitol and the West Wing of the White House were evacuated.

At 10:05 A.M., the south tower of the World Trade Center collapsed.

At 10:28 A.M., with most of the world watching on television by this time, the World Trade Center's north tower collapsed.

14

At 10:48 A.M., officials confirmed that United Airlines Flight 93, flying to San Francisco from Newark, New Jersey, had crashed eighty miles southeast of Pittsburgh.

Throughout the morning and later in the day, government buildings around the country were evacuated. The United Nations closed. Financial markets were closed. Except for rescue workers, lower Manhattan was evacuated.

At 5:20 P.M., World Trade Center Building 7 collapsed.

And at 8:30 P.M., the President of the United States addressed the nation.

When we live through an experience like that, certain dramatic images are branded into our memories forever, images of horror and heroism.

The image of those planes slamming into those buildings; we'll never forget that.

The image of those buildings coming down like they had been imploded, and our knowing what that meant; we'll never forget that.

The image of people frantically running away from the buildings while rescue workers and firefighters and police officers and chaplains were running into the buildings to try to save lives. And as we now know, many of those brave officials lost their own lives in the process. We'll never forget that. And then there is the image of

15

search dogs looking for signs of life in the rubble. When they found good news, they barked and wagged their tails; when they found news that was not good, they moaned and cried.

We'll never forget the image of people rushing to blood centers all over the country and standing in line for three to five hours to give blood; the image of families gathering in homes, waiting and waiting for some word about the fate of their loved ones who were in harm's way that Tuesday morning; and the image of courageous people using cell phones from the backs of hijacked planes and from the top stories of burning buildings to call their loved ones to say, "I may not make it out of here, so I want to tell you I love you."

There is the image of the changing of the guard at Buckingham Palace, with the British band playing our national anthem rather than theirs, the image of people from nations all across the world bringing flowers to our embassies and participating in candlelight vigils, and the image of American flags flying everywhere, showing the world that we will stick together as a nation.

And of course, the image of people all over America making their way to their churches to kneel at the altar and pray; we will never forget that.

These graphic images reminded us—and will continue to remind us—how we all felt under attack. As we think about the people in those buildings and on those airplanes, as well as their loved ones, their pain becomes our pain, because after all is said and done, we in this nation are a family.

Leonard Pitts Jr., in his column in *The Miami Herald,* wrote these words the day after the attack:

What lesson did you hope to teach us . . .?

Did you want to tear us apart? You just brought us together. . . .

We are a vast and quarrelsome family . . . but a family nonetheless. . . . We are fundamentally decent . . . peace-loving and compassionate. We struggle to know the right thing and to do it. And we are, the overwhelming majority of us, people of faith, believers in a just and loving God. . . .

Indeed, we are strong in ways that cannot be measured by arsenals. . . .

Yes, we're in pain now. . . . We'll go forward from this moment sobered, chastened, sad. But determined, too. Unimaginably determined.

When President George W. Bush addressed the nation on the evening of September 11, he wisely quoted verses from Psalm 23, including these words: "Even though I walk through the valley of the shadow of death, I [will] fear no evil, for you are with me" (v. 4 NIV). That is the good news of our faith—that God promises to be with us always and that nothing can separate us from God and his love.

The apostle Paul, writing to the church at Rome, said much the same thing. He wrote, "What shall we say to these things? . . . [N]either death, nor life, nor angels, nor rulers, nor things present, nor things to come, nor powers, nor height, nor depth, nor anything else in all creation, will be able to separate us from the love of God in Christ Jesus our Lord" (Romans 8:31, 38-39, paraphrase).

That is what we as Christian people hold on to right now. That's the promise we wrap our arms around now. That's the promise we stand upon now—the promise of God to be with us always come what may, to walk with us through the hard valleys of life, and to bring us to the mountaintop on the other side. So when we are under attack as individuals, as a church family, or as a nation, that's what we do. We keep walking forward, one day at a time, knowing that God will always be with us, and God will see us through.

Now, let me be more specific with three thoughts.

First of All, Because God Is with Us, We Walk in Faith, Not Fear

That Tuesday morning, as I sat at my desk and watched the television news unfold this horrible, tragic nightmare that set our world reeling and broke our hearts, all kinds of questions flooded my mind:

Why did this happen?
How could this happen?
Who could do a thing like this?
What does this mean?
Who is responsible?
How do we respond?
How can we help?

All these questions were tugging at my heart, when suddenly my mind darted back to a poignant story of courage. It was the story of a young man whose wife had died, leaving him with a small son. Home from the cemetery on the day of her funeral, they went to bed as soon as darkness came because there was nothing else that man could think of that he could bear to do. As the young man lay in the darkness, brokenhearted, grief-stricken, numb with sorrow, the little boy broke the stillness from his bed with a heart-wrenching question: "Daddy, where is Mommy? When is she coming back?"

The father tried to get the boy to go to sleep, but the questions kept coming from his confused child's mind. After a while, the father brought the little boy to bed with him. But the child was still disturbed and restless, and the probing, painful questions kept coming. Finally, the little boy reached out his hand through the darkness and placed it on his father's face, asking, "Daddy, is your face toward me?" Assured verbally and by his own touch that his father's face was indeed toward him, the little boy said, "Daddy, if your face is toward me, I think I can go to sleep." And in a little while, he was quiet.

The father lay in the darkness, and then he, with child-like faith, lifted up his own needy heart to his Father in heaven and prayed something like this: "O God, the way is dark right now, and I confess that I don't see my way through; but if your face is toward me, somehow I think I can make it."

This is our faith, isn't it? God is with us. His face is toward us, and his presence supports us when we have nowhere else to turn. As the American author and poet Ralph Waldo Emerson put it, "What lies behind us and what lies before us are tiny matters compared to what lies within us."

That's number one: Because God is with us, we walk in faith, not fear.

Second, Because God Is with Us, We Walk in Hope, Not Despair

Late in the evening a few days after September 11, I was watching television. Someone was interviewing a young man who had survived the World Trade Center attack. He had worked in the south tower. He told of how someone had come to his floor of the building and shouted, "Something bad has happened in the north tower! Everybody out! Get out as fast as you can!"

He started down the stairs. As he reached the lower floors, the second plane rammed into his building. The young man was knocked to the floor, all the lights went out, and there was smoke.

He had no idea what had happened, but he knew he needed to get out of there. However, in the darkness, he became confused, disoriented, and terrified. He was holding on to the wall in the blackness.

Suddenly, he felt a hand on his shoulder. It was a policeman. The policeman said, "Follow me. I know the way out." And the policeman took his hand and led him to safety. In the interview, the young man said, "You can't imagine the incredible relief I felt when that policeman said, 'Follow me. I know the way out.'"

This is what the Christian gospel says to us: "Here is One who knows the way out—the way to safety and life.

Here is One who can save you, and that is our hope." Because God is with us, we walk in faith, not fear, and we walk in hope, not despair.

Third and Finally, Because God Is with Us, We Walk in Love, Not Hate

Everything about the September 11 attack was horrendous. The most despicable aspect of that evil assault was that it was a heartless, surprise attack on innocent people, a hateful, cruel attack on innocent civilians who were going about their daily routines with no place to take cover and no way to defend themselves. We were outraged by this hateful act, and our hearts cried out for justice; indeed, the leaders of our nation and our world began working together immediately to this end.

When people join together and commit a terrible crime, what do we do? We find those people and deal with them in such a way that they cannot strike again. That is justice. Our God is a God of justice and *love*. God wants *us* to be a *people* of justice and love. So we must resist the temptation to stereotype and label whole nations, peoples, and religions as guilty, because when we do that, we make the same mistake—morally speaking—as those who attacked us on September 11. They attacked us because somebody had carefully taught them to hate.

22

At noon on the Friday after the attacks, our church congregation gathered in the sanctuary for the National Day of Prayer and Remembrance. I asked them to walk through the hard valley lying before us while holding on to two symbols—the eagle and the cross. Our nation chose the eagle as its symbol because it is the only bird not afraid of the storm. The cross is the great symbol of our Christian faith because it reminds us of the power of love, and it reminds us of God's victory over sin and evil and death.

That is why we can be courageous. That is why we need not be afraid. That is why we can face the troubles of the world with strength and confidence and with trust in God. Because God speaks not from an easy chair, but from a cross—as One who suffered and endured the worst the world can dish out and was victorious over it! That's what the cross means: God wins! God's goodness cannot be defeated. God's truth cannot be silenced. God's love cannot be defeated. It is stronger than hate.

That's the good news: Ultimately God wins, and he wants to share the victory with us. So, because God is with us, we go forward. Because God is with us, we walk in faith, not fear. We walk in hope, not despair. We walk in love, not hate.

"GOOD RELIGION, BAD RELIGION"; HOW DO YOU TELL THE DIFFERENCE?

Matthew 17:1-8

I received a powerful E-mail message from a friend of mine, Jim, who is a lawyer. He was writing to say that our worship service on the Sunday after the September 11 attacks was one of the most helpful and meaningful services he had ever attended. There were two reasons for that: First, it was a service that had touched his heart profoundly, as we in our church family supported one another in the painful aftermath of the previous week's events. Second, the service was powerful to him uniquely because of where he was on the morning of September 11.

He and three friends were in a business meeting in a company dining room on the sixty-sixth floor of the south tower of the World Trade Center. Jim was sitting on the side of the table that faced the window. Suddenly he saw an American Airlines jetliner coming toward the building. He said to his friend, "That plane is flying way too low." Everybody turned to look, and they saw the wings rocking back and forth. The pilot appeared to be struggling to get control of it. Someone said, "That plane is going to crash!"

The plane passed by about fifteen or twenty stories above them and went out of view, and then there was a tremendous explosion that shook the room. Jim and his friends ran to the window, and they saw debris raining down—an unbelievable shower of debris. As they looked up, they could see that the north tower of the World Trade Center was on fire.

At this point, Jim and his friends didn't know precisely what had happened, but they knew they needed to get out. They told everyone they saw to evacuate, and then they took the elevator down to the forty-fourth floor. There, they discovered that the express elevators to the lobby were not operating, so they rushed to the stairs and started walking down.

Making his way down, Jim called his wife on his cell phone to tell her that he was okay but that a plane had collided with a building. She was watching the story on television and explained to Jim what had happened. She said,

"They are saying that a small private plane crashed into the north tower." "No," Jim said, "it was a commercial jetliner—a *big* plane. I saw it."

More and more people were rushing into the stairwell now. When Jim and his friends reached the thirty-fourth floor, suddenly the building rocked violently. Jim said he couldn't imagine what would cause a building that large to rock like that. He wondered if it could have been an exploding fuel tank from the plane that had hit the north tower.

As they moved further down the stairs, they saw people who had been injured. Coworkers and rescue workers were helping them. Finally, they got to the lobby. There was a lot of smoke, and a lot of debris had piled up on the plaza outside.

Police officers and security officers were there, directing people not to go out, but to go down through the subway station. Jim and the others went below and moved across the train platform to a set of stairs that led above ground a block or so north of the World Trade Center. People were moving up and out intentionally, as quickly as they could, but no one panicked.

When they came up to street level, the area where they surfaced was jammed with people. They all were looking up at the burning buildings. That was the first time Jim and his friends saw the gaping hole in the north tower and the fire blazing out of the south tower not too far from where they had been meeting only thirty or so minutes before. More (much more) had happened than they had realized.

Jim used his cell phone again. He called his wife to tell her that he was out and okay. She told him about the second plane. Along with the rest of the nation and our world, Jim was shocked, stunned, and heartsick.

Police were shouting to people now, telling them to go north. In the pandemonium, Jim and his friends were separated. Jim found an off-duty cab driver and convinced him to take him and some others uptown. While driving, the cab driver had his radio on. They heard about a third plane that had hit the Pentagon and then the report that the south tower (where Jim and his friends had been) had collapsed. Jim turned to look out the rear window of the cab and saw that the south tower was gone from the skyline. Later, the north tower came down. Jim knew what that meant. He thought about his own brush with death and about all those innocent people who weren't so fortunate, who didn't make it out.

He rented a car and drove to Texas. He and his wife came to our 8:30 A.M. worship service that Sunday. While worshiping with us, he and his wife and his cousin passed a package of tissues among them, dabbing the tears from their eyes, realizing how precious and how fragile life can be. Jim commented that one thing he had learned from the experience was that every day is a gift from God, and it ought to be lived with that fact firmly and gratefully in mind.

I was sharing Jim's story with some friends when one of them said, "How could anybody hijack a plane, crash it into a building—killing thousands of innocent people—and call that *holy*?"

That's what I want us to examine together now. How do you distinguish between "good" and "bad" religion? "Good religion," "bad religion"—how do you tell the difference?

A few days after September 11, I heard James Fleming discuss this topic of good and bad religion. Dr. Fleming is a brilliant Bible scholar, a bright archaeologist, and an outstanding Holy Land tour guide. He lives in Jerusalem for six months each year, and he has a fascinating perspective, especially with regard to Christianity, Judaism, and Islam. Dr. Fleming says that if you study these three major religions closely, you will discover that the vast majority of the Christians, the Jews, and the Muslims of the world are peace-loving, law-abiding, compassionate people. But then, within each of the three, there are radical groups that "get off the track" and "go off the deep end," becoming militant extremists.

Dr. Fleming also says that these extremists, wherever they appear, have three things in common—three commonalities. First, they are closed-minded. They do not permit thinking or questioning or discussion or dialogue. They tell you what their scriptures say, and they tell you that you must accept their version with no interpretations and no discussion. They tell their followers, "Here's what the scriptures say for you to do, and if you go against this, you are going against God." But a close examination will show that the extremist leaders have twisted and distorted their scripture to make it fit their own agenda. That's why they don't want any questions.

A second commonality of these extremist groups is that they have no room for women in leadership. They go overboard to keep women "in their place." The extremists do everything they can to keep women from having equal rights. Anybody or any group that encourages equal rights for women is seen by the extremists as an enemy, a threat.

A third commonality of these extremist groups, as Dr. Fleming mentioned, is that they have one human leader who has total authority over their lives. He tells them what to wear, what to eat, what to do, and whom to marry.

Now, these are the three commonalities that Jim Fleming listed. Let me add a fourth one: Religious extremists have no tolerance or respect for anyone outside their group. They teach their followers that everybody not in their group is the enemy, that it's them against the world, that everybody outside their group is an adversary.

But even worse than all of this, the extremists do something even more destructive: They teach their followers to hate. All of that together makes for bad religion, and bad religion can produce terrorists.

The point is clear: Religion can be very, very good; but misdirected, it can be very, very bad! When religious ideas are faithful and true, they save, they heal, they make whole, they give new life. But when they are twisted and false and all mixed up, they crush, they destroy, they devastate, they kill.

Some people think that it doesn't matter what you believe as long as you believe *something*. But let me tell you, *it does matter*. It matters more than you can imagine! We saw the awful, painful evidence of this on September 11, 2001. Good religion, on the one hand, is beautiful and creative and constructive, and it empowers people to do godlike things. Bad religion, on the other hand, is disastrous, and it produces fanatics who are narrow and negative and intolerant, and sometimes even cruel. Let me sum this up by underscoring three basic qualities of good, healthy religion.

First of All, Good, Healthy Religion Encourages You to Think and to Grow

Cult leaders and radical extremists try to close the book on truth. They say, "Don't think. I will think for you. I will tell you what the scriptures say. I will tell you what to believe and what to do, and anyone who questions me will be disciplined severely." But how wrong that is!

Healthy faith is always open to new truth from God. A call to discipleship is a call to grow in the faith, to think, to stretch, to wonder, to discuss, to dialogue, to probe, and to love God with our minds.

Remember what Jesus said to Peter on the Mount of Transfiguration (Matthew 17:1-8). Peter, James, and John had gone through an incredible spiritual mountaintop experience, and Peter was so inspired that he wanted to stay there, but Jesus said to him, in effect, "Peter, this has been good, but we can't stay here. We must move on. We must be open to new experiences with God, at other times and in other places."

Healthy faith keeps moving and learning. Someone once said, "A mind is like a parachute: It works best when

31

open." Good religion is like that as well. It keeps stretching, ever open to new truth from God, while the extremists of bad religion want to close the book on truth and shut down thinking. That's number one: Good religion keeps growing.

Second, Good Religion Works Now, in Practical Daily Living

Underscore the NOW! Good religion gives us confidence and inspiration for living *now*. It makes us better people *now*! Now, of course we believe in heaven. Of course we believe that nothing—not even death—can separate us from God and his love. But good religion is not just an insurance policy for another day, not just an escape hatch to get us out of this world.

Look at what Jesus did when he came down from the Mount of Transfiguration. He went right down into the valley and healed a little boy who had epilepsy. This means that healthy faith is not just something that dwells on the past or longs for the future, but works *now*, speaks to us *now*, strengthens us *now*, and makes us whole *now*.

Remember that great line from the movie *As Good as It Gets*? Jack Nicholson's character says to Helen Hunt's character, "You make me want to be a better man." That's what good religion does for us. Indeed, that's what Jesus Christ does for us. He makes us want to be better persons.

Since September 11, many people have asked, "Why would people agree to suicide missions?" Well, it's because somebody has led them to believe, taught them to believe, convinced them to believe that if they perform this act, they will receive instant immortality and all kinds of rewards in the afterlife. But you see how wrong this is. If religion is nothing more than an insurance policy for heaven and has no effect on how you live morally now, and how you treat others now, then something is wrong. That is bad news and bad religion.

Good religion and healthy faith encourage us to keep growing and learning and thinking, and it works now in practical, daily living.

Third and Finally, Good Religion Makes You More Loving

It inspires us to reach out in compassion and in service to others. On the other hand, many cults and extremists teach their followers the opposite—that everybody outside of their group is the enemy. But look at what Jesus said about this. For Jesus, *love* was the real measuring stick for healthy faith. In the Bible, the words "love" and "faith" are often used interchangeably: walk in faith, walk in love; put on faith, put on love. In the Bible, love is underscored over and over as the most genuine, the most reliable, and the most authentic sign of mature discipline.

Remember how Jesus put this in John 13: "I give you a new commandment, that you love one another. Just as I have loved you, you also should love one another. By this everyone will know that you are my disciples" (vv. 34-35). And remember how the songwriter expressed it later: "And they'll know we are Christians by our love, by our love. Yes, they'll know we are Christians by our love" (Peter Scholtes, "They'll Know We Are Christians by Our Love," 1966).

Also remember how dramatically the apostle Paul put it. His message to the Corinthians was essentially this: What does it matter if you can speak in tongues? If you don't have love, it's not worth anything. And what does it matter if you can do miraculous things? Without love, it's all empty and worthless. And what does it matter if you can spout high-sounding theology into the air? Without love, it's only so much noise. Faith, hope, love abide; these are the things that endure. Of these three, the greatest is love. So put love first. Make love your aim. That's what God wants you to do (see 1 Corinthians 13).

Listen very closely now. If you have a religious

experience that makes you more loving, then it is likely a valid experience; it is healthy faith. But if you have a religious experience that makes you narrow or hateful or judgmental or "holier than thou," then, in my opinion, that is bad news and bad religion.

Now, let me conclude with this thought. You want to know what good religion looks like? Then look at Jesus! He is the pattern, the blueprint, the measuring stick for genuine, healthy faith. The poet John Greenleaf Whittier put it like this:

> Our Lord and Master of us all!
> Whate'er our name or sign,
> We own Thy sway, we hear Thy call,
> We test our lives by Thine.
> . . . .
> We faintly hear, we dimly see,
> In differing phrase we pray;
> But, dim or clear, we own in Thee
> The Light, the Truth, the Way!
>
> ("Our Master," 1866)

3
WHY IN THE WORLD DO THE INNOCENT SUFFER?

Romans 8:35-39

There's an E-mail message that began making the rounds in recent days after September 11. It's called "What a Difference a Day Makes." Have you seen it? There were several versions of it. Here is one of them:

On Monday, we E-mailed jokes.
On Tuesday, we did not.

On Monday, we were fussing about praying in school.
On Tuesday, we would have been hard-pressed to find a school where someone was not praying.

On Monday, our heroes were athletes.
On Tuesday, we relearned who heroes are.

On Monday, there were people trying to separate us by race, sex, color, and creed.

On Tuesday, we were all holding hands.

On Monday, we were irritated that our rebate checks had not arrived.

On Tuesday, we gave money away gladly to people we had never met.

On Monday, we were upset that we had to wait five minutes in a fast-food line.

On Tuesday, we stood in line for three to five hours to give blood for the dying.

On Monday, we argued with our kids to clean up their rooms.

On Tuesday, we couldn't get home fast enough to hug our kids.

On Monday, we went to work as usual.

On Tuesday, we went to work, but some of us didn't come home.

On Monday, we had families.

On Tuesday, we had orphans.

On Monday, September 10, life felt routine.
On Tuesday, September 11, it did not.

What a difference a day makes.

As we reflect upon the heart-wrenching tragedy of September 11, one of the big questions that haunts us and screams inside us is: Why?

Why do horrible things happen?

Why do good people suffer?

Why are the innocent victimized?

Why does God let bad things happen to good people?

The horrific events surrounding that day raised the question again, but it is not a new question.

I remember sitting in a hospital waiting room with a young woman who was struggling with that question. The doctor had just brought bad news about her husband, and she felt utterly forsaken. "Doesn't God care?" she cried. "Why my husband? He has been a good man, a wonderful father, a good churchman. He has been honest and kind and loving. Now he has to die young, while people who have never done anything for anybody, who have never been to church, who have cheated and lied, live on. Why? It's just not fair!" She cried as she buried her face in her hands.

I certainly would not presume to know the full answer

to the problem of human suffering. It is without doubt one of life's great mysteries. It is a problem so deep, so profound, so wrapped around with holy awe that from the beginning of time, people have pelted heaven with their prayers, asking, "Why?" The wisest person in the world cannot answer that question completely. And yet, it seems to me that we ought to take a shot at it; we ought to try. Somebody, somewhere, should say something in answer to this bothersome question: Why do good people suffer?

Out of my struggle with this perplexing question comes a list of some helpful ideas—four basic thoughts, outlined in a similar way by Harry Emerson Fosdick in his book *Dear Mr. Brown: Letters to a Person Perplexed About Religion* (New York: Harper & Row, 1961; chap. 7). Let me list them, and then we can walk through them together. Why do good people suffer? First, because we live in a world of dependable natural laws; second, because we live in a world that is wracked with growing pains; third, because we live in a world of risky relationships; and fourth, because we live in a world of freedom of choice.

First, People Suffer in Our World Because We Live in a World That Has Dependable Natural Laws

As Jesus put it, the rain falls "on the just and on the unjust" (Matthew 5:45 RSV). In other words, the natural laws of the universe are dependable. They are unbending. They operate the same for all people. They are no respecters of persons.

Take the law of gravity, for example. If a little baby stands up in his or her high chair and falls off, the law of gravity, as Fosdick suggests, is merciless. If Billy Graham and I climbed to the top of a church steeple and jumped off, goodness or morality would not be a factor of our surviving the jump. The fact that he is a much better man than I am, the fact that he has done more good things than I have, the fact that he is more valuable to the world than I am, does not enter into or affect the outcome. We both would be seriously hurt or killed because we had violated this dependable, unbending law of gravity.

Here is another example. A good man climbs a mountain. He has been a faithful Christian all of his life and is active in the church. But he loses his footing and falls a thousand feet to his death. The fact that he had an outstanding record in living would make no difference at all to the law of gravity. It works for good and bad alike. There is no distinction. In this particular case, its working caused a tragedy.

Cause and effect, cause and consequence, are bound together in dependable, unbending succession; and much of our suffering comes from running head-on into the dependable laws of the universe.

40

We live in a cause-and-effect world, with dependable natural laws that give order to creation, that make medicine possible, that make engineering possible, that make farming possible, that make learning and scientific advances possible, and that make all human progress possible; but which also can bring suffering when violated.

Jesus spoke about our cause-and-effect world. The tower of Siloam fell, killing eighteen people, and Jesus was asked in the Gospel of Luke, "Why? Whose fault was it? Who was to blame?" (13:4-5). And Jesus said, in effect, "It's nobody's fault. Those people just happened to be standing in the wrong place when the tower fell." In a sense, that's what happens to us; sometimes we suffer because we happen to be standing in the wrong place when a law of the universe falls on us or when we have put ourselves in a position where the laws work against us rather than for us. But it has to be that way. We must have dependable laws or we couldn't live.

Consider the alternatives. If the laws of nature were suddenly repealed, your preacher's pulpit might fly up to the ceiling one Sunday morning, and your church pews might slide out the window. You might fall down and be unable to get up. Your car might go upward or sideways. Our world would become complete chaos. You couldn't

41

count on anything. As Dr. J. S. Whale put it, "If water might suddenly freeze in midsummer; if the specific gravity of lead might at any time become that of thistledown; if pigs might fly or the White House turn into green cheese—[our] life would be a nightmare" (as quoted by Fosdick in *Dear Mr. Brown*, p. 70).

So in spite of all the pain and suffering that our world's natural laws might bring upon us, few, if any, of us would want to see them go away; we simply could not live without them.

Move with me to the second idea.

Second, People Suffer Because We Live in a World That Is Wracked with Growing Pains

We live in a world that is in the process of becoming, a world that is still developing, still unfolding. Or, to put it bluntly, we live in a world where we don't know everything yet, and what we don't know hurts us! We are wracked with growing pains. We learn by trial and error, and sometimes our errors come back to haunt us. You see, the truth of the matter is that we are doing things right now that are harmful to us—things that are causing suffering—and we don't even know it. There are so many things we don't know yet, and what we don't know hurts us.

Let me illustrate this. Several years ago, I helped our daughter Jodi study for a science test. I was intrigued by something in her science textbook—namely, the fact that not too many years ago, we didn't know about the existence or nature of germs. Lacking that medical knowledge, surgeons didn't scrub up as they do today. During operations, they wore unsterilized coveralls (like those of an auto mechanic), because no sensible doctor wanted to soil his clothing with bloodstains. Doctors didn't wash their hands before delivering a baby, and they had no idea that not washing could cause the deaths of many babies and mothers.

Here's another example. Rent a movie made in the 1940s. What do you notice? Everybody's smoking cigarettes. At the time, they didn't know that smoking is harmful to your health. Just think of it—the millions of people who have lost their lives, and those who are losing their lives today, through ignorance, through what we don't know, through what we have not yet learned about living in this world. We are supposed to be living in the Age of Knowledge, but don't you wonder what future generations will say about us and the things we didn't know, or the things we are doing now through which we unwittingly bring about our own suffering. We are living in a world wracked with growing pains.

43

I'm sure that God could have made a "finished product." God could have made a finished universe, as Fosdick says, one that is "perfect, static, all-complete, with nothing more to be done in it" (*Dear Mr. Brown*, p. 70). But we wouldn't like that at all, would we? We would be bored stiff. The zest of living is in the discovery, the new findings, the growing, the learning, the surprises. Christopher Morley wrote a poem about this, "No Coaching," that goes like this:

I went to the theatre
With the author of the successful play.
He insisted on explaining everything.
Told me what to watch,
The details of direction,
The errors of the property man,
The foibles of the star.
He anticipated all my surprises
And ruined the evening.
Never again!—
The greatest Author of all
Made no such mistake.

(*Translations from the Chinese* [New York: George H. Doran Co., 1922])

I think it is true that we live in a world of surprises, a world of learning and discovery; and some of our suffering comes from the fact that we live in an unfinished world, a world wracked with growing pains.

Here's a third idea.

Third, We Suffer Because We Live in a World of Risky Relationships

We are a relational people. God made us that way. He made us so that we are not merely separate, isolated individuals; instead, as Fosdick says, we "are woven together, by loyalty, love, mutual need and interdependence, into homes, friendships, communities" (*Dear Mr. Brown*, p. 71), and, I might add, we are also woven together into churches and nations. Fosdick goes on to say that "this fact of inescapable fellowship is the source of [both] our deepest joys and our most heartbreaking tragedies" (p. 71).

Almost every joy we know of in life involves the element of risk.

If I choose to love you, I am running the risk that you may reject me and break my heart. But love is worth the risk.

If you make a new friend, you run the risk that your friend may be false to you. But friendship is worth the risk.

If you have children, you run the risk that they may let you down and cause you a lot of heartache and sleepless nights. But children are worth the risk.

If I drive a car, and even if I obey every rule of safety, I still run the risk that someone else may run a traffic light or drive recklessly and smash into me. But every day, I take that risk.

When Jesus called Judas to be a disciple, he ran the risk that Judas might turn on him and betray him. But still, Jesus took that risk.

Risky relationships are woven into the very fabric of life in this world. The more deeply we love, the more deeply we can be hurt. Much of the suffering in our world today comes from these risky relationships—between persons, groups, and nations. And yet, we would not want to miss out on the joys of love just because we are afraid of being hurt. It's worth the risk!

Now here's the fourth idea.

Fourth, We Suffer Sometimes Because We Live in a World That Gives Us Freedom of Choice

When God made us, he did not make us helpless puppets dangling from strings. He made us free. He gave us free will, freedom to choose our own way. But we sometimes make wrong choices and bring suffering on ourselves and on others.

For example, a man decides that he can beat a train to a crossing, and he misses by only one second. But still, he misses.

A teenager tries drugs on a dare and over time becomes a drug addict.

A diplomat says the wrong thing, and two nations that have been friends for years find themselves at war.

A boy runs away from home to the far country, and a father's heart is broken.

A teenage girl with a bright mind and a brilliant future drops out of high school because she has to get married.

A group of terrorists choose to crash jetliners into crowded buildings, and thousands of people lose their lives.

A group of men jealous and resentful of a teacher from Nazareth decide that he is a threat to their way of life. So they nail Jesus to a cross.

Our greatest gift in life is the gift of freedom, but how we have misused it! So much of the world's suffering comes from the ignorant or wicked or confused or selfish, sinful misuse of our free will.

Fosdick put it this way:

> All the way from intimate personal hurts and tragedies to the vast catastrophe of war, how much of human agony

springs from the personal choice of evil instead of good!
What Caliban said to Prospero in *The Tempest*,

You taught me language; and my profit on't
Is, I know how to curse,

the whole world, in one way or another, is saying today,
You taught me physics and my profit on't is, I know how
to make the H-bomb; you taught me flying and my profit
on't is, I know how to destroy whole cities.

(*Dear Mr. Brown,* p. 71)

Yes, much of our suffering comes from bad choosing,
from misuse of our free will. We choose to hurt rather
than to help, to hate rather than to love, to punish rather
than to forgive. We choose littleness rather than bigness
and sin rather than Christ. We suffer because we live in a
world of dependable, natural laws, because we live in a
world that is wracked with growing pains, because we
live in a world of risky relationships, and because we live
in a world where we have freedom of choice.

There is one more thing to be said about suffering in
our world, and that is the good news of our faith—namely,
that we are not alone. God is with us, enabling us to
suffer creatively, enabling us to turn our defeats into vic-

tories and our sorrows into triumphs. We can trust God. We don't have to be afraid because nothing can separate us from God and his love.

You see, God speaks not from an easy chair, but from a cross, as one who endured the worst suffering this world can dish out and was victorious over it. Remember how Leslie Weatherhead put it: "The cross felt like defeat to Jesus and looked like defeat to the disciples and was called defeat by the world. Yet it was God's greatest victory" (Ralph W. Sockman, *The Whole Armor of God* [New York: Abingdon Press, 1955], 34).

This is the good news of Christianity: No matter how many painful "Good Fridays" come our way, they are always followed by a victorious Easter morning.

4

How Firm a Foundation

Matthew 7:24-28

Bishop Charles Jordan spoke at the 2000 General Conference of The United Methodist Church in Cleveland. He told a touching story that came back to my mind in the painful aftermath of the terrorist attacks of September 11.

Bishop Jordan's paternal grandparents were born into slavery in Alabama. Later, they were moved as slaves to Mississippi, and that's where they were on the day of emancipation. The bishop's grandmother was in the cotton field, picking cotton, when word came that all slaves were now set free. Bishop Jordan's grandfather found his wife in the field and said, "Virginia, Virginia! I've got some important news for you. Great news! You won't believe what has happened!" She kept working. "Stop!"

he said. "Wait a minute! Listen to the news that's just come."

She kept working because it wasn't time to stop, and no overseer had given instructions to stop. Her husband walked beside her and said, "Virginia, listen to me. We are free! We are free!" Still, she kept working. It didn't register. "Virginia," he said, "did you hear what I said? Our prayers have been answered. We are free! We have been set free!"

The impact suddenly hit her, and she fell to the ground and cried. She sobbed and sobbed and sobbed. Bishop Jordan's grandfather let his wife cry for a bit, and then he gave her their instructions: "We have to go up to the main house for a meeting. They are going to tell us there what to do." Then he reached down to help her up. "Come on, Virginia, let me help you to your feet. Let me help you up." "No," she said. "You come down here with me. We are going to get on our knees together and thank God for the gift of freedom and pray for the strength and the guidance to use our freedom well."

Isn't that beautiful? Look at her words again. She said, "We are going to get on our knees together and thank God for the gift of freedom and pray for the strength and guidance to use our freedom well." This is the constant challenge for those of us who are privileged to live in a free land: to remember that freedom is a precious gift, and to pray that we will use our freedom well.

But how do we do that? Where do we find the strength and guidance to use our freedom well? The answer, of course, is to remember the firm foundation on which our nation was built and to steer clear of those shaky, unstable foundations that can bring the house down. Jesus told a parable about this at the end of the Sermon on the Mount. He said that if you build your house on a rock-solid foundation, it can withstand any storm. But if you build it on shifting sands, your house will come down, and great will be the fall of it.

I am by nature an optimist. And I am optimistic about our future in America. But one concern I have is what we have done to the concept of the separation of church and state. As never before, we are being pushed to think that separation of church and state means to silence the church, to ignore the church, to steer the church away from any direct contact with the state, and to weaken the moral influence of the church.

"Religion and politics don't mix," they say loudly, over and over and over. "Freedom of religion means freedom *from* religion," they imply. But that is contrary to the original intention of the separation of church and state principle.

Remember that the early founders of America came from England, and in the England they knew so well, the church and state were pretty much the same. The church of England and the state of England were so interwoven that the state told the church what to do, and the church lost its moral and spiritual influence. It was a puppet of the state.

Early American leaders saw this was not good. They envisioned a nation *not* where the church would be silenced by the government, but where the church could have a voice, where the church could be empowered to influence the government for good, where the church could be enabled to stand tall and speak out freely for goodness and righteousness, and where the church could be encouraged to be the conscience of society.

President George Washington, in his farewell address to the nation, said this:

Of all the dispositions and habits, which lead to political prosperity, Religion and Morality are indispensable supports. In vain would that man claim the tribute of Patriotism, who should labor to subvert these great pillars of human happiness, these firmest props of the duties of Men and Citizens. . . . [L]et us with caution indulge the supposition, that morality can be maintained without religion. Whatever may be conceded to the influence of refined education on minds of peculiar structure, reason and experience both forbid us to expect, that national morality can prevail in exclusion of religious principles.

(from Boston's *Independent Chronicle,* September 26, 1796)

And John Adams said: "We have no government armed with power capable of contending with human passions unbridled by morality and religion. . . . Our Constitution was made only for a moral and religious people."

Abraham Lincoln is reported to have said: "My concern is not whether God is on our side; my great concern is to be on God's side. . . ."

Years later, when Peter Marshall was chaplain of the United States Senate, he prayed: "Lord . . . help us see that our liberty is not the right to do as we please, but the opportunity to please to do what is right."

What were these great Americans saying? They were saying that we must remember our roots, we must remember the firm foundation on which our country was built, and we must remember that a democracy will work only if there is morality and goodness in the land. The noted political philosopher Montesquieu once spoke about this. He said that dictatorships work only when the people are afraid of their leaders, that monarchies work only when the people respect and venerate their royal leaders, and that democracies work only when the people are good and virtuous and righteous and loving and honest.

I believe those virtues are of God. They are written boldly in the Ten Commandments and underscored dramatically in the teaching of Jesus. It is apparent to me that they were at the heart of the American Dream from the very beginning, and they will withstand any storm and endure to the end of time.

Let me bring this closer to home with three quick thoughts that outline what should be our firm foundation as a free nation, three thoughts that can empower us to use our freedom well.

First of All, In God We Trust

Those words, *In God We Trust,* were first placed on U.S. coins in 1864. And while the phrase has been our nation's official motto only since 1956, the belief behind it was present long before then. In fact, trusting God as our sure foundation has been a central part of our heritage from day one. It held our leaders together. It motivated them. It inspired them. It undergirded them. They wanted to build a better life, they wanted freedom, and they wanted to forge a new nation in a new land. They believed that God was with them somehow and that God was in it all.

That's our heritage as a nation, as a church, and as

individuals: partners with God, working for a better world. Those are our roots! And those roots we need to pass on to our children. I saw a bumper sticker the other day that said this well: "God above all, or chaos over all."

Several years ago, someone said to the great minister Phillips Brooks, "Dr. Brooks, you always seem so serene and confident. Why is that? What is your secret?" Phillips Brooks gave a simple but profound answer to that question. He said, "I am a Christian!"

That's our faith, isn't it? That's our "blessed assurance." We do our best and trust God for the rest. We live each day trusting God and knowing that come what may—no matter how dark the outlook may be sometimes—ultimately, virtue will win! Goodness will win! Righteousness will win! God will win!

That's what we hold on to, especially now, in this post-September 11 world. That's what we wrap our arms around. That's the promise we stand upon: God is with us, and ultimately, God will win.

That's the first thought: In God we trust.

Second, In God We Hope

Recently, a good friend sent me a fascinating E-mail. It was entitled "The New Short Version of the Bible—the Bible in 50 Words." Here is how the message read:

God made
Adam bit
Noah arked
Abraham split
Joseph ruled
Jacob fooled
Bush talked
Moses balked
Pharaoh plagued
People walked
Sea divided
Tablets guided
Promise landed
Saul freaked
David peeked
Prophets warned
Jesus born
God walked
Love talked
Anger crucified
Hope died
Love rose
Spirit flamed
Word spread
God remained.

That's pretty good, isn't it? The key words of Christian hope are those last two words: *God remained!* The world tries to silence God. The world tries to crucify God. And people try in more sophisticated ways to do that today.

But, you see, the good news is that God can't be silenced; God can't be killed; God can't be buried. He resurrects! He rises again! God remains! That is our hope, and that's what we need to hold on to with both hands.

In God we trust, and in God we hope.

Third and Finally, In God We Love

When I was in seminary, I had a classmate named Paul. Paul had an amazing experience in the 1950s as a U.S. soldier in Korea. One night while on a scouting patrol, Paul wandered above the 38th Parallel, into enemy territory. He was captured and became a prisoner of war. The experience was horrible beyond words. And as a result of his imprisonment, Paul became the victim of amnesia. He could not remember anything. He did not know who he was, where he was, where he had come from, or what he was doing there. He didn't even know his own name.

Day after day, night after night, hour after hour, he tried desperately to remember something from his darkened past. Finally, two words came: "Our Father." Just those two words. He didn't know what they meant, but he knew they represented something from his past. So he repeated those two words: "Our Father, our Father, our Father," hoping that more memories would come back to him.

Well, something else did come, and he remembered: "Our Father, who art in Heaven." Then he repeated that phrase over and over, until he remembered the words "hallowed be Thy name." His memories continued to come back until he had reconstructed the entire Lord's Prayer. And then he remembered his parents, who had taught him the prayer. And then he remembered his church, his neighborhood, his country, his mission there, and finally, he remembered his name!

Isn't that something? Paul rebuilt his life and his memory around the Lord's Prayer, starting with those first two words, "Our Father." Paul not only survived that experience, but also ironically came out of it with two things he never had before: a call to the ministry and a photographic memory.

Now, I don't want any of us to have to go through what Paul went through, but wouldn't it be something if every one of us could rebuild our lives around the two words "Our Father"? If starting right now, we could see every person we meet as a brother or sister who shares with us the same heavenly Father ("Our Father") and for whom

Christ died, we would see that person differently. We would speak to that person differently; we would relate to that person differently; we would treat him or her differently; and it would change our city, our nation, and our world.

How can we use our freedom well? By remembering our roots, our firm foundation, and by remembering that it is in God we trust, in God we hope, and in God we love.

5

WHEN YOU FEEL
COMPLETELY STRESSED OUT

Numbers 11:13-17

A few years ago, I was asked to lead a workshop at a national convention for schoolteachers. The topic they assigned me was an interesting one: "How to Cope with Stress Creatively!" When I arrived at the convention center, I was told to go to the main lobby and check in with the registrar. The registrar was a large, powerful, take-charge woman who looked and acted very much like a person who would be equally at home as a professional wrestler or as a drill sergeant for a U.S. Marines boot camp. She was barking out orders authoritatively, and her assistants were jumping to obey her commands. Finally, she turned her attention to me. "You!" she said, "Step over here!"

I said what anyone in his right mind would have said in that moment—"Yes ma'am"—and I stepped over in front of her. When I told her my name, she said, "I've been looking for you. You're going to have the biggest group. We have sixty-three different workshops for the teachers to choose from, but you will have twice as many in your group as any of the rest."

Before I even had a chance to swell with pride, she quickly added, "Now, don't go getting the big head, because the big attendance has nothing to do with *you*!" "Oh?" I said quizzically. "No," she said, "it's not you. It's your *subject*! If we want to get the teachers out for a workshop, all we have to do is use either the word *stress* or the word *cope*. And *you've* got *both* of them in your title, 'How to Cope with Stress Creatively!' The teachers will come running to that because they feel 'stressed to the max' these days, and they need all the help they can get."

She was right. I did have a large group, and it quickly was obvious that they were indeed feeling great stress on the job.

Those teachers are not alone. No question about it. These are stressful times. Since September 11, many people have felt stressed to the breaking point. Many have felt pulled apart at the seams. We all know what it feels like to be "stressed to the max."

62

Some writers these days would have us believe that stress is a modern-day problem caused by the hectic, pressure-packed, and violent world in which we live. Yet, though we quickly would agree that there are indeed new stress factors today caused by the frantic pace and hard demands of our contemporary, competitive, volatile world, it is also true that stress is as old as the Bible.

Did you know that, of all people, Moses, at one point, felt stressed to the limit? That is precisely what the passage in Numbers 11:13-17 is all about.

Moses had had it. He was trying his best to lead his people out of Egyptian slavery to the Promised Land, and he was "up to here" with their problems and complaints. He was suffering from burnout. The red flags were obvious. He was feeling overworked and underappreciated. He was tired of the pressures, the demands, the responsibilities, and the burdens of leadership, and he was bone-weary with all of the griping and groaning and criticizing. Everything was going wrong.

Their problems fell neatly into three categories. For one thing, they were having a hard time reaching their destination. It took them forty years to travel from Egypt to the Promised Land, a distance of only about two hundred miles—approximately the distance from Houston to San Antonio. So short a way to go, so long a time to get

63

there. (Moses' wife said that it took forty years because Moses would never stop and ask for directions!)

And they ran out of food, so God had to give them something called *manna* to eat. (Nobody knows for sure what manna is, but the author Garrison Keillor said that *manna* is Hebrew for "tuna casserole!") They got lost, ran out of food, and complained. *Why did you do this to us, Moses? We were better off as slaves in Egypt! Why didn't you just leave us alone?* the Israelites complained. Finally, Moses stressed out, and he turned to God for help.

This brings us to our Scripture in Numbers 11:

> So the LORD said to Moses, "Gather for me seventy of the elders of Israel, whom you know to be the elders of the people and officers over them; bring them to the tent of meeting, and have them take their place there with you. I will come down and talk with you there; and I will take some of the spirit that is on you and put it on them; and they shall bear the burden of the people along with you so that you will not bear it all by yourself." (vv. 16-17)

What an amazing passage this is! Even though it was written thousands of years ago, its message is as fresh as the morning sun. Look at the practical advice here. Stress is the result of carrying too much weight in your life. Ask any doctor or engineer. They will tell you about that if you put too much stress on a component or limb, you soon will see stress fractures.

So as we try to deal with the stress caused by the tragedy and horrors of September 11, let's take this practical advice from the Old Testament and apply it to our lives today. This text in Numbers 11 gives us a simple and yet profound three-count formula to use when we feel completely stressed out. Let me show you how it works.

First of All, When You Feel Stressed Out, Let Your Friends Help You

Delegate some of the burden to other people. That is exactly what God told Moses to do. Don't try to carry it all yourself. Share the load with others. Let your friends help you; that's what friends are for.

Several years ago, a group of American theologians traveled to Africa to visit Albert Schweitzer at his jungle hospital on the Ogowe River. The theologians spent three days with Dr. Schweitzer and were greatly moved by the experience and by the unique privilege of spending time with this giant of a man.

One event, however, stood out in a special way. It was close to noon and extremely hot. The group was walking up a steep hill with Dr. Schweitzer, who was eighty-five years old at the time. Without warning, Dr. Schweitzer broke away from the group and made his way across the slope of the hill to a place where an African woman was struggling upward with a huge armload of wood. The American theologians watched with admiration and concern as the eighty-five-year-old Albert Schweitzer helped the woman carry that heavy load up the hill.

When they all reached the top of the hill, one of the Americans asked Dr. Schweitzer why he did things like that, implying that in that extreme heat and at his age he should not do such things. Dr. Schweitzer smiled, and then, pointing to the woman, he said simply, "No one should ever have to carry a burden like that alone."

That's what God was saying to Moses during the exodus: *This is too big a load for any one person to carry. It's too stressful to try to do this all by yourself. Let your friends help you.*

That's number one: When you feel "stressed to the max," delegate some of the burden to other people. Let your friends help you.

Second, When You Feel Stressed Out, Let Your Church Help You

When Moses was almost ready to throw in the towel, God said to him: "Go to the tent of meeting" (which was essentially their church). Some folks go about it all wrong. They are under stress and stay away from the church. "Let me get my act together, and *then* I'll get back in church," they say. But that's not the way it works. It's the church that can help us get our act together.

On the evening of September 11, people all over our nation and our world made their way to their places of worship. They wanted and needed to be in church, they wanted and needed to pray, they wanted and needed the strength and reassurance that comes from faith. They wanted and needed to be in the presence of God. We had taken a blow to the heart. We wanted and needed the encouragement that only God and the church can provide.

It was December 17, 1979—a Monday morning and just a week before Christmas—and I was rushing to get ready for work. We had a big staff meeting that morning, and we had so much to do to get ready for Christmas. But then the phone rang. My wife, June, answered it in the kitchen. I could hear her talking to someone but could not make out the words. Suddenly I heard her running down the hallway toward the master bedroom, and I knew something was wrong. But nothing could have prepared me for what she said: "Jim, get on the phone quick. It's your sister, Susie, calling from Winston-Salem. Your mother was killed in a car wreck this morning!"

I couldn't believe it. We had lost our father in a car wreck years before, and now Mother (so full of life and love) was suddenly gone! We had the funeral on that Thursday morning in Memphis. We stayed through the weekend to handle the business matters of her estate, and then we flew home on Monday afternoon. We landed at 3:00 P.M. on Christmas Eve. We rushed home and put our bags in the house. The Christmas Eve Communion service was scheduled for 5:30 P.M. We were expecting twelve hundred people for that service, and I had told the staff I would be there.

Just before we left for church, I looked quickly through the mail—all those letters and sympathy cards touched me deeply—and then I saw it and knew immediately what it was: a big box with a Winston-Salem, North Carolina, postmark. I opened it, and I was right. There were our Christmas gifts from my mother, carefully selected and beautifully wrapped and mailed to us the day before she died. It blew me away, and I said, "I don't know if I can do this tonight. I don't know if I can hold together." "You don't have to," my family said, "we'll call the church and tell them you won't be there." But I said, "No! I need to go. They need my help, and besides, I need to get back in the stream of life."

I'm so glad I went because something happened that night that never happened to me before or since. It was like the whole congregation had rehearsed this. Every

68

worshiper, from the smallest child to the oldest adult, did the same thing. There were hundreds of people, and every one of them did the same thing: With one hand, they reached for the bread of Holy Communion, and with the other, they tenderly touched and patted my hand. You're not supposed to talk during Communion, but they were speaking volumes with that touch by saying, *We are with you and we are going to get you through this. We are going to put the heart back into you.*

Holy Communion was never more holy for me than that night, and time stood still because those precious people, by the grace of God and in the Spirit of Christ, had created for me a powerful moment of encouragement. That's a powerful memory for me because it illustrates how the church can help and heal and strengthen and reassure. In his letter to the Galatians, the apostle Paul put it like this: "Bear one another's burdens, and in this way you will fulfill the law of Christ" (6:2).

When you feel stressed to the max, let your friends help you, and let your church help you.

Third and Finally, When You Feel Stressed Out, Let Your God Help You

Comedian Richard Pryor spent the early years of his professional career trying to get ahead, trying to make money, trying to be a success. But then one day, in a terrible situation, he was critically burned. For days and days he fought for his life in the hospital. The doctors did not know if he would make it or not. He hung in the balance between life and death for some time. Finally, he did pull through, he did survive, and he did recover. Shortly after being released from the hospital, he made his first public appearance since the accident, on *The Tonight Show,* with Johnny Carson. Richard Pryor told Johnny Carson that when you are critically ill like he was, money suddenly is not important anymore. When in such dire circumstances, he said, "You know, you don't call on the Bank of America to help you. You don't call on nobody but God."

This is the most crucial thing to remember about this amazing passage in Numbers 11. Moses felt "stressed to the max." So he called out to God, and God was there! God heard his cry, and God helped him.

When you feel totally stressed out, don't try to carry that burden all by yourself. Let your friends help you, let your church help you, and most important of all, let your God help you.

6
REAL LIFE IS
IN THE TURBULENCE

Matthew 11:2-6

We have a close friend named Paul. He and our son, Jeff, have been best friends since they were five years old, and over the years Paul has been like family to us. Paul is a ministerial student at a theological school as well as a student intern at his church. And my family and I were fortunate enough to hear him preach one Sunday morning a few years ago.

In his sermon, Paul talked about a conversation he had had earlier in the summer with the senior pastor. The senior pastor explained to Paul that due to a vacancy on the church staff, they needed Paul to be the interim youth minister until they could locate someone permanent.

One week later, Paul found himself with a bunch of senior-high-age young people, getting ready to go white-water rafting down the Ocoee River near Chattanooga, Tennessee. Paul said he supposed this activity fell in his contract under the phrase "other duties as assigned." Most people were very excited and looking forward to the trip (especially the kids), but Paul was not! He dreaded this white-water rafting experience for three reasons: "First," he said, "I don't like to swim at all. Second, I don't like to be cold at all. And third, I have seen the movie *Deliverance!*"

Things got worse when the guides arrived. Most of them were seasoned veterans. One man had been a river guide for over twenty years, and in all that time his raft had capsized only twice. But did Paul and his group get him for their guide? No. They got "Fuzz."

Fuzz was a free-spirited college student who had been a river guide for less than a week. Paul said that as soon as he saw Fuzz, his first thought regarding the river mission was, "Abort! Abort!" It turned out to be an unforgettable experience, but Paul still has not recovered mentally, emotionally, or physically. They rafted Class 3, 4, and 5 rapids. For those of you who have never been rafting, that means bad, *real* bad, and real, *real* bad! Paul fell out of the raft three times. The water was freezing, and as

72

he was bouncing around in the rocks and the rapids, he said that he felt like a human pinball machine. And, he said, he was thinking unchristian thoughts about Fuzz and about the senior minister. After the second fall, he said he came up out of the water and was sure that he saw vultures circling overhead!

Paul said that the third time he fell out wasn't his fault. About five miles into the trip, Fuzz, for no apparent reason, did a weird thing. Right in the middle of a Class 4 rapid called "Hell's Hole," Fuzz stood up in the raft, jumped straight up into the air, and disappeared into the river. He was gone—life jacket and all.

Meanwhile, Paul and the young people, deserted by their guide, had to navigate "Hell's Hole" all alone. They didn't make it. They flipped over pretty quickly, and all fell into the river. About a minute or so later, Fuzz shot back up out of the water, not too far from where he had jumped in. Well, it was complete chaos and absolute pandemonium. Two other rafts had to come to the rescue to pull Paul and Fuzz and all of those young people out of the rapids.

When everybody was safely on the riverbank, Paul asked Fuzz, "What in the world were you thinking?" Fuzz said, "You don't understand; that's the best part of the river. That's where the vortex is."

Fuzz explained it like this: Right at that point in the river, the water churns like a water tornado. The vortex is like the eye of the storm. If you can jump out just right and hit the vortex, even with your life jacket on, you can drift peacefully to the bottom in eight feet of water. Fuzz said, "It's amazing. It's so peaceful down there. There is turbulence all around you, but there in the vortex, its so peaceful and calm and serene."

Now, let me tell you something about the vortex. You can stay down there as long as you want to—except for one thing: You can't breathe there! At some point, no matter how great the sensation, you have to leave the vortex and come up for air, and the way you do that is you step back into the turbulence, and it shoots you back up to the surface, and you can breathe again. The vortex feels pleasant for a short while, but if you stay there, you will suffocate. The only way to survive is to get back into the turbulence.

Ever since I heard Paul's sermon, I have thought a lot about Fuzz and the vortex. The truth is that many people go through life like that—looking for the vortex, even if it means deserting the people they are responsible to and for, trying to escape the turbulence of life, trying to find that quiet, serene place where all is calm and peaceful. Many of us want that and long for that. We are looking for "the vortex." We dream of that safe place that's protected from the turbulence, from the hardships, challenges, and problems of the world. And the bad news is that we can find it pretty easily—or at least we think we can—in drugs, alcohol, extramarital affairs, or even programs that offer serenity in an easy, quick-fix plan of "$19 down and $19 a month." But the problem is, the vortex isn't real. There *is* no lasting vortex! And even if there were, no matter how great the sensation may feel in the short run, it never, ever lasts! At some point, you have to come up for air. You can't stay there. If you do, you will smother; you will suffocate.

So, the point is clear: Real life is in the turbulence. Now, of course, we all remember that even Jesus had moments when he needed quiet time, time apart, time away, time to meditate and think and pray. But—don't miss this—he didn't *stay* there. He came back to live in the turbulence. He came back to help people with their hurts, their struggles, and their problems.

That's what this Scripture passage is about in Matthew 11. John the Baptist had been arrested by King Herod and was thrown into prison, and John was tired of the turbulence of life. He wanted Jesus to hurry up and bring a new kingdom, to zap the Romans quickly with his power, and to create a new era of peace and prosperity and tranquillity.

John the Baptist and Jesus were cousins, and Cousin John got a little impatient with Jesus. He wanted Jesus to hurry up and lead them to some quiet, calm, serene vortex. So, John sent his disciples to Jesus with a pointed question that only one cousin would ask of another: "Are you the one who is to come, or are we to wait for another?" (Matthew 11:3). In other words, *What are you waiting for? When are you going to get with the program? Why don't you hurry up and establish this kingdom for which we have all been longing and waiting?*

Look, now, at how Jesus answered the disciples of John the Baptist. He said, "Go and tell John what you hear and see: the blind receive their sight, the lame walk, the lepers are cleansed, the deaf hear, the dead are raised, and the poor have good news brought to them" (Matthew 11:4-6). What was Jesus saying to John? Simply this: Real life is in the turbulence. The Kingdom is not found in some safe, comfortable nest, insulated from the problems of the world. The Kingdom is the power of love reaching out to those who are needy, to those who are sick, to those who are broken, and to those who are hurting, and bringing them help and hope and healing. *That's* where the Kingdom is. That's where the breath of real life is!

Jesus was saying to John, "Look, John, I am bringing the Kingdom, but it's not a kingdom of wealth and clout and military might. It's not a kingdom of calm repose and tranquillity, hidden away from the struggles of life. No, it's a Kingdom of love and sacrifice and service to others. That's where real life is found—not in the vortex, but in the turbulence."

Let me show you what I mean with three thoughts.

First of All, Real Life Is Found in the Turbulence of Daily Living

Real life is not found so much in the arrival at some longed-for destination, as in the excitement and the challenges and the opportunities of the journey. And when we learn that, it changes our lives. When we learn that, it enables us to embrace life with both hands. But somehow we get it mixed up. We get duped into thinking that real life is "out there," somewhere. It's somewhere off in the distance, and we long for it, look for it, wish for it, dream of it. And while we are doing all that longing and looking and wishing and dreaming, life passes us by! Life happens, and we miss it!

A friend recently sent me an article that puts it well. I don't know who wrote it, but it has a great title—"Dance Like No One's Watching"—and it has these words:

We convince ourselves that life will be better after we get married, have a baby, then another. Then we are frustrated that the kids aren't old enough and we'll be more content when they are. After that we're frustrated that we have teenagers to deal with. We will certainly be happy when they are out of that stage. We tell ourselves that our life will be complete when our spouse gets his or her act together, when we get a nicer car, are able to go on a nice vacation, when we retire.

The truth is, there's no better time to be happy than right now. If not now, when? Your life will always be filled with challenges. It's best to admit this to yourself and decide to be happy anyway. One of my favorite quotes comes from Alfred D. Souza. He said, "For a long time it had seemed to me that life was about to begin—real life. But there was always some obstacle in the way, something to be gotten through first, some unfinished business, time still to be served, a debt to be paid. Then life would begin."

At last it dawned on me that these obstacles were my life. . . . So, treasure every moment that you have. And treasure it more because you shared it with someone special, . . . and remember that time waits for no one. . . .

Happiness is a journey, not a destination.

> Thought for the day:
> Work like you don't need money,

Love like you've never been hurt,
And dance like no one's watching.
—Anonymous

This is precisely what Jesus was underscoring in Matthew 11: Real life is *now*! So, seize it with both hands; embrace it with both arms; love it with all your strength; celebrate it with all your heart.

That's number one: Real life is not in some tranquil vortex cut off from the world and its problems. Real life is found first of all in the turbulence of daily living.

Second, Real Life Is Found in the Turbulence of Unselfish Service

Broadly speaking, there are two kinds of people in the world: sick people and healthy people. The sick people go miserably through life saying, "For God's sake, *love* me." And the healthy people go happily through life saying, "For *God's* sake, let me love you."

You want to be happy? You want real fulfillment? You want real life? Here's how you find it: Go find somebody in need today, and help that person. Go find somebody hurting today, and comfort him or her. Go find somebody struggling today, and encourage that person.

In the book *The Cherry Log Sermons* (Louisville, Ky.: Westminster John Knox Press, 2001), Fred Craddock tells about an experience he had a few years ago when he was the visiting preacher at a church. On that Sunday afternoon, a van pulled up in the church parking lot, and a group of young people got out. They were a ragtag-looking group—tired and dirty and sweaty and rumpled. "What is this?" Dr. Craddock asked. The answer came, "Oh, they are members of our church. They have been on a missions work project." Those young people joined with others, and in one week they had built a little church for another community. The young people were exhausted. They were sitting on their sleeping bags, waiting for their parents to pick them up. Dr. Craddock went over to one of the boys and said, "Are you tired?" The boy said, "Am I tired? *Whew!* Oh, *man*, am I tired!" Then he said, "But this is the *best* tired I've *ever been*."

Why did he say that? Because he had been out there in the turbulence of the world, unselfishly helping others, reaching out to others, serving others, sacrificing for others, making a difference for others.

That's what Jesus was doing and talking about in Matthew 11. Real life is found not in some sheltered cocoon, far away from the stress factors of the world. Real life is found in the turbulence—in the turbulence of daily living and in the turbulence of unselfish service.

Third and Finally, Real Life Is Found in the Turbulence of Sacrificial Love

A few years ago, an article appeared in *The Columbus Dispatch* that dramatically shows what real love is all about. The article read like this:

> When Frank Steger pushed himself into an upright position in the hospital bed, the heart monitor's fluid cursive line disintegrated into an erratic scribble. . . .
>
> "Thirsty," he complained. [His wife Mary] lifted the straw to his lips as he pulled the oxygen mask aside. The medicine made him sick then. She fetched the basin, wrapped a firm arm around his spasm-wracked shoulders, mopped the sweat from his forehead.

Further describing the gentle and thorough care of the wife for her terminally ailing husband, the article goes on to read:

> In the end, love comes down to this; . . . "Help me sit up." . . . Not the smoldering glance across the dance floor. . . . It is the squeeze of a hand. I'm here. I'll be here, no matter how long the fight. . . .

Now, let me ask you something. Do you know what it is to love like that? Do you love anybody like that? You can't live in a vortex and love like that. Jesus Christ came into the world to teach us the real meaning of love. He showed us in a manger; he showed us with his healing touch; he showed us on a cross, that real love is sacrificial, self-giving, generous love. And Jesus showed us that that's the way God meant life to be lived—not in some secluded, isolated vortex, but rather in the turbulence of daily living, in the turbulence of unselfish service, and in the turbulence of sacrificial love.

7

UNITED WE STAND

Acts 2:43-47

Have you heard about the telemarketer who phoned a home late one afternoon? A young boy answered the phone with a whispered "Hello." And then this conversation took place:

"Hello! What's your name?"

Still whispering, the little boy said, "Jimmy."

"Well, how old are you, Jimmy?"

"I'm four."

"Good. Is your mother home?"

"Yes, but she's busy right now."

"Okay, is your father home?"

"Yes, but he's busy, too."

"I see. Well, who else is there?"

"The police."

"May I speak to one of them?"

"They're busy also."

"Any other grownups there?"

"The firemen."

"May I please speak to a fireman?"

"They're all busy."

"Jimmy, all those people in your house, and I can't talk with any of them? What on earth are they doing?"

In a still-whispering voice, little Jimmy said, "They're looking for me!"

The truth is that people all over the world are looking for something. It's called connectedness! Whether they realize it or not, they are looking for a sense of belonging, a sense of acceptance, a sense of inclusion, a sense of *connectedness*—with God and with other people. And when it happens, it is so beautiful. Let me show you what I mean.

Here in Houston on Wednesday, June 22, 1994, the Houston Rockets basketball team defeated the New York Knicks in the seventh and final game of the NBA Championship. What a night it was for the Houston Rockets and their fans! What a night it was for the city of Houston and the state of Texas! What a night it was for me personally to be there, thanks to the kindness of a good friend who gave me a ticket, to experience firsthand that special *kairos* moment.

It was thrilling to see the Rockets win the first world championship for the city of Houston in a major sport. It was thrilling to see Hakeem Olajuwon named the most valuable player and then to hear Hakeem quickly remind us that while individual awards are nice, basketball is a *team* sport.

All of that was thrilling, but I saw something happen that night that thrilled me even more, namely, the way that event brought people together, connected people, bonded people, united people. The walls that so often divide people came down that night, and we became ONE. Class didn't matter. Color didn't matter. Cultural background didn't matter. Houston Rockets fans were united. If only for a moment, we became *one*! Let me describe it for you.

Seated next to me on my left was a bright young man who is a member of our church. He had just completed his first year at SMU.

On my right was a huge African American man who looked like he could play offensive guard for any pro football team. Actually, he was from New York but was a Houston Rockets fan and came all the way from

Manhattan to see the game and root for the Rockets. Next to him was a prosperous-looking couple who was celebrating their thirty-fifth wedding anniversary.

Behind us there were a middle-aged Asian couple and a white-haired great-grandmother with her ten-year-old great-granddaughter, whose face was painted with Houston Rockets symbols.

We were a diverse, eclectic group—a smorgasbord of humanity—and yet in that moment, all the barriers came down, all the prejudices vanished, all the differences went away, and we were united. We became one! Throughout the game, we talked strategy, cheered loudly, jumped up and down, and shared hugs and high fives. And then, when the final buzzer sounded and we won the game, it was beautiful bedlam. The big guy from New York got so excited that he grabbed me with both of those massive arms, and he hugged me so tightly that he lifted me off the ground and was flopping me around like a rag doll. Then he dropped me to the ground and high-fived the great-grandmother. The Asian couple and the anniversary couple were hugging each other, and the college student and the great-granddaughter were jointly holding up a sign that read "Champ City!"

It was great! It was thrilling—not just to win the game (nice as that was), but also to see diverse, divergent, different people being drawn together and made one. As I witnessed and experienced that powerful and touching moment of unity, I found myself thinking: *Why can't it be like this all of the time?* I wanted so much for that spirit of love and acceptance and unity to continue and grow and flourish—to bond like that, to unite like that, to see people of all different backgrounds connecting like that. I want that so much for our city, our church, our nation, and our world.

When we stop and think about it, that's what America at its best is all about. We are the United States, *E Pluribus Unum*—"Out of many, one"—one people indivisible, one nation under God, with liberty and justice for all. We are connected, bonded, united. That kind of "oneness" is a beautiful thing, and when it happens, we can know that somewhere in heaven God is smiling because that's the way God wants it to be.

Now, that is precisely what happened at Pentecost. All those people from different places, of different cultures, with divergent languages and colors and customs—they were all drawn together by the power of the Holy Spirit, and they became ONE! Remember how the Bible puts it: "They were all together in one place" (Acts 2:1).

But the question is, how does that happen for us? How does God unite us and connect us and hold us together?

What are the things that bring us together and stick us together and keep us together? There are many, but for now, let me underscore three of them. I'm sure you will think of others. But for now, let me get you to try these on for size. Here's number one.

First of All, There Is a Shared Commitment

To become a great team, a great church, a great nation, a united people, one necessary ingredient—one key essential—is a shared commitment. Commitment to the dream is so important. A commitment so deep that people will serve and sacrifice for it is vital. That kind of shared commitment draws people together, bonds them, unites them, connects them.

Several years ago, we were looking for a new minister for our staff. We needed a person with special training for this key, specialized job. One man came in for an interview, and we were so impressed with him at first. He was bright, talented, capable, eloquent, personable, and very well trained for this specific position. He had three degrees. All was going well in our conversation until he said, "Jim, you know from our dialogue and my résumé what I do well. So, let me tell you what I don't do!" And then he said, "I don't do night meetings! I don't do committees! I don't do Saturdays! I don't do retreats! I don't do weddings or funerals! I don't do manual labor! And I don't do janitorial work!"

Now, would it surprise you to know that he didn't get the job? No way! Because the call of the church is to service and sacrifice, to unconditional commitment, to do whatever it takes for the kingdom of God.

Put that over against this. Leonard Sweet once overheard a young seminary student complaining about his new appointment—that it didn't fit his talents. Sweet wondered what the world would be like now if certain historical figures had said, "I don't do that." For instance, what would have happened if Michelangelo had said, "I don't do ceilings," or if John Wesley had said, "I don't do preaching in fields." Image how much better the world is because Mary didn't say that she didn't "do virgin births" or Jesus crosses.

In our nation, we could add another one to that list: The world is a better place because the early leaders of America didn't say, "We don't do *freedom*." They didn't say, "We don't do declarations of independence." No; they took a stand! They stood united for freedom and justice for all. They believed that God was with them, and they were committed to the dream that is still our hope as a nation today. It was true at Pentecost, and it was true at Philadelphia. It's true today in Washington, and it's true where *you* live. It's true in our nation and in the church. God uses the glue of a shared commitment to draw people together and to hold them together.

Second, There Is a Shared Adversity

After the Houston Rockets won the NBA crown in 1994, local radio broadcaster Gene Peterson kept shouting, "How sweet it is! How sweet it is!" The victory was sweet, not just because they won the title, but because of all the adversity they had faced and overcome as a team on the way to the title. After the game, the players and coaches all said pretty much the same thing: "It's a great feeling to win, because we have worked so hard and been through so much together." Adversity helped make them a team. Adversity helped them connect and bond and unite.

It's true not just in sports, but also uniquely with old soldiers. Have you ever seen old war veterans come together after having been apart for many years? It's like "old home week." They hug one another and tease one another and call one another nicknames. They reminisce and share old war stories. They have a special kinship because they went through adversity together in days gone by.

It's also true in families. Noted marriage expert Gary Smalley tells of interviewing hundreds of close-knit, happy families, trying to find the one thing that pulled them together. Interestingly, many of those families said that one thing, for them, was camping! Gary Smalley said that further research revealed that it wasn't really the camping that drew these families together, but the adversities produced by camping together as a family. There is something to that. When your family gets together, what is it that makes you laugh and feel close? Probably it is some shared adversity.

Gary Smalley goes on to say that one of the moments his three children love the most is the time he built one of those exercise machines that hangs you upside down by the feet. Gary Smalley built this contraption in the garage and bolted some old shoes to the top of it. He climbed up, slipped into the bolted shoes, and then let himself hang upside down. He stayed hanging there so long that he did not have the strength to pull himself back up. He was stuck there, trapped, and in a near panic. But then the children (all teenagers) came home, and he thought, "Great! I'm saved!"

Well, the first thing the children did was fall on the floor, laughing. The second thing they did was run to get the camera. Next, they took lots of pictures and exacted all kinds of promises from their dad. Finally, they got him safely down, and that moment of adversity became one of the great moments the children remember in their family's history: *"Hey, Dad, remember that time you were trapped upside down?" "It's great to be coordinated, isn't it, Dad?" "Some families have upside down cake, but we have upside down DAD!"* Gary Smalley says that when they face some adverse situation now, they say, "This is tough, but just think, we are bonding!"

It's true in families, in friendship, in nations, and in churches. We are drawn together and united by a shared commitment and a shared adversity.

Third and Finally, There Is a Shared Love

One day, out of the blue, a physical education teacher received a letter from a former student named Lou. Lou wanted that teacher to know what a great impact the teacher had made on his life, so he wrote these words to his former teacher:

> I remember the first day I had you for P.E. . . . We all had to run the 600-yard dash, and I didn't want to. I was always coming in last, no matter how hard I ran (and I always ran as hard as I could). But this one [time] was different.
>
> . . . I remember you running along side of me that last 100 yards, yelling, "Good effort, Lou! Great effort! Absolutely magnificent. . . ."

I felt like I'd won the Olympic Gold Medal for the marathon. And I became totally devoted to you because no one had ever encouraged me like you.

The next year I was your manager for the soccer team, a position I took [again the following year]—despite the fact that you had left to circumnavigate the globe—but left the next year to play fullback for the JVs—when you returned.

And I would never [have] had the courage to do it, if it had not been for your example.

Well, that was more than a decade ago. I went to college and majored in journalism because my senior English teacher told me I had no ability as a writer. . . . All through those four years I held your example in my mind, looked for possibilities and wondered—often— how you always managed to be so positive all the time.

Five years ago I met Jesus and figured you out.

(Tim Hansel, *You Gotta Keep Dancin'*, [Elgin, Ill.: D. C. Cook Publishing Co., 1985], 135.)

What unites people in a meaningful and lasting way in a nation, in a family, in a church? God does, through a shared commitment, a shared adversity, and a shared love.